THEORY I

THEORY I

End Your One-Minute Search For Excellence

**RICHARD E. THOMPSON, M.D.
AND DAVID R. THOMPSON**

SENSS, INC.

Library of Congress Catalogue Card Number 86-090531
ISBN   0-940555-00-X

Copyright © 1986 by SENSS, Inc.

Published by SENSS, Inc.
P.O. Box 47603
San Antonio, Texas 78265

All rights reserved. No part of this publication may
be reproduced or transmitted in any form or by any means,
electronic or mechanical, including photocopy, recording
or any information storage and retrieval system,
without permission in writing from the publisher.

Illustrations by Cynthia T. Allen

First printing: December 1986.
Second printing: March 1987.

Printed in the United States of America

What they're saying about THEORY I

I don't know whether to laugh or cry. These 70 rules really describe my boss!
   —*Richard's Secretary*

I always knew they'd do something important.
   —*David's Mother; Richard's Wife*

I never heard of it.
   —*Lee Iacocca*

How to use this book

If You Are An Executive or "Middle Manager"

Use this book any way you want to. As a paperweight ... to support your lower back ... to swat mosquitoes.

Except—
Don't read it! Do not buy books to *read*. You have no time to read and understand. You are a manager.

We suggest displaying this book prominently with your other management-style books. Except Machiavelli. Unlike Lee Iacocca's book and Tom Peters' books, Machiavelli's book likes dark, secret places.

That's it. Put Machiavelli in the bottom, left drawer of your desk. Lock the drawer.

Swallow the key.

If You Are Not A Manager

Impossible.

Everybody must manage—

- their assigned work

- their time
- their own advancement
- their boss.

You can use **Theory I** principles in your daily life, even if you do not have a "management position."

If You Are A Customer

You're the one who really needs this book. Learn to protect yourself from **Theory I** managers and employees.

Contents

Foreword	*xiii*
Introduction	*xvii*

Chapter 1
IMPATIENCE AND INSENSITIVITY

Rule 1	Worship the fast track	3
Rule 2	Never believe, "Things take time"	4
Rule 3	Influence, control, and authority are synonyms	5
Rule 4	Ignore pleas for humanism in business	6
Rule 5	Employees are not people	7
Rule 6	Never listen to employees	10
Rule 7	Discourage innovative underlings	11
Rule 8	Be inconsistent	12
Rule 9	Use every situation to your own advantage	13
Rule 10	Today's bottom line is the only consideration	14
Rule 11	Ignore learning to write better letters and memos	16
Rule 12	Jump on bandwagons	17
Rule 13	Be insensitive	18
Rule 14	Never listen to consumers	19
Rule 15	Always be on the phone	20

Chapter 2
NEGATIVISM

Rule 16	That's not my job	25
Rule 17	Always be critical	27
Rule 18	Use **Theory I** methods to communicate criticism	28
Rule 19	Subordinates are inferior	29

Rule 20	Don't be distracted by productivity and quality	30
Rule 21	Force compliance with company policy	31
Rule 22	Never appreciate and enjoy what you have	32
Rule 23	Always be defensive	33
Rule 24	Always be secretive	34
Rule 25	Truth in advertising has no market value	36
Rule 26	Never admit a mistake	37
Rule 27	Stupid questions don't deserve an answer	38
Rule 28	Follow the GGG Credo	39
Rule 29	The Golden Rule is religious only	40
Rule 30	Live by the Mobile Golden Rule	41

Chapter 3
SUPERFICIALITY

Rule 31	The successful business relies on a computer	45
Rule 32	Money is the only motivation	46
Rule 33	Oppose tax reform	47
Rule 34	Sweat the small stuff	48
Rule 35	Expect "the system" to work	49
Rule 36	Expect "communication" to be automatic	50
Rule 37	Never have one person do what four people can	51
Rule 38	If a form is confusing . . .	52
Rule 39	Create the illusion . . .	53
Rule 40	Let the logistics beat you	40
Rule 41	Beware of promises . . .	56

Rule 42	Create a consumer expectations gap	58
Rule 43	When the consultant leaves, photocopy and adopt	59
Rule 44	Don't read	60
Rule 45	When faced with lack of productivity . . .	61
Rule 46	Never do in a conference call . . .	62
Rule 47	Beware of old-fashioned definitions of "work"	63
Rule 48	Always look busy	64
Rule 49	If the method doesn't work, attack the concept	65
Rule 50	Go through the motions	66

Chapter 4
ARTIFICIALITY

Rule 51	When it comes to your title . . .	75
Rule 52	Never call a spade a spade	76
Rule 53	Let television dictate your lifestyle	77
Rule 54	Apply sports maxims directly and absolutely	78
Rule 55	Never communicate directly	79
Rule 56	Believe in the adversary process	80
Rule 57	The corporate myth isn't just for tax purposes	81
Rule 58	Take a bureaucratic approach to any task	82

Chapter 5
NERDNESS

Rule 59	Solve your problem, not the customer's	85

Rule 60	Wait for complaints before making adjustments	87
Rule 61	To get more money, threaten disruptive action	88
Rule 62	Loyalty has no market value	89
Rule 63	Be arrogantly aggressive	90
Rule 64	If "no" doesn't work, show your muscle	91
Rule 65	Nerdness can be corporate	92

Chapter 6
Ego

Rule 66	Beware of people who answer your questions	97
Rule 67	Travel like you mean it	98
Rule 68	Never worry about your arrogance . . .	99
Rule 69	Gatekeepers, use your power	101
Rule 70	Above all, never evaluate your own performance	102

Afterword	*103*
An Alternative	*104*
THEORY I *Glossary*	*105*

Foreword

Managers are not the only crazy people in the world. But managers as a group seem to have a leg-up on everyone else. Whether disciples of Iacocca, Mary Kay, or the world according to Peanuts, managers usually find a way to screw up. Managers start in search of Excellence, but decide Mediocrity isn't so bad because it's less work. Few managers understand that "one-minute manager" doesn't mean the total time in an average work day. A manager's concept of leadership is to start in the front row of the Michelob Marathon.

Are we being over-critical? Does our satire border on sarcasm?

Sure. Otherwise, this book is not controversial, and we'll never appear with either Johnny Carson *or* Joan Rivers.

On the other hand, if there's no truth in what we say:

- Why does "international competition" mean foreign trade embargoes to protect a shoddy product, instead of meaning dependable, quality products which compete successfully?

- Why do marketing divisions of companies promise more than operations divisions can deliver?

- Why is the executive's busy day at the office:
  - Filing a lawsuit against one's closest competitor
  - Breaking a strike
  - Revising the Five-Year Plan in Year One because it's not working
  - Creating insecurity in employees?

- Why are many chief executive officers and middle managers compulsively revising their résumés?

- Why is a 53% employee turnover rate the acceptable norm?

- Why do we consider hypothetical causes of decreased productivity when the real cause is people don't work while they're at work?

What Would You Do?

You may ask, "What would *you* do?"

Funny you should ask.

The obvious answer is one more "management-style" book.

So . . . Welcome to the winner's world of the Consumer Expectations Gap, Going Through The Motions, Nerdness, Sweat The Small Stuff, and the Mobile Golden Rule . . .

THEORY I.

Introduction

What Is THEORY I?

Theory I management has six basic principles:

- I Impatience and Insensitivity
- N Negativism
- S Superficiality
- A Artificiality
- N Nerdness
- E Ego

embodied in the following seventy (70) tongue-in-cheek rules.

Chapter 1

Impatience and Insensitivity
nsane

RULE 1

Worship the fast track

Don't worry about the horse being blind. Just load the wagon.
—*John Madden*
CBS Sports Commentator

Time spent with others to help them understand the company's goals and your expectations is not productive time.

Caution: Some managers try to be fast-track, but fall short. Whether a customer or an employee, there's nothing worse than dealing with a half-fast manager.

RULE 2

Never believe, "Things take time"— this is an excuse

Plant the seed today; expect the blossom tomorrow. No blossom, fire the seed.

RULE 3

Influence, control, and authority are synonyms

Someone may tell you:

- People in positions of authority may have little control because they don't know how to influence others

  and

- People who may be good at influencing others have more control than those in authority.

The **Theory I** experts agree: Avoid people who talk this way. They might control you by influencing you, even though they have no authority.

RULE 4

Ignore pleas for humanism in business

Example:

American management in the past has been singularly blind to the needs of human beings. Management wants to eliminate the human equation from business . . . (American management) says, 'How could you do business by making a friend? What's that got to do with the bottomline?' As it turns out, it has everything to do with it.

—*Edward T. Hall*
   Business Consultant; Author, *The Silent Language*. Former Professor of Anthropology, Northwestern University, Evanston, Illinois

Quoted in the *Chicago Tribune,* July 28, 1985. Copyright 1985, American Association for the Advancement of Sciences, excerpted from *Science '85,* distributed by Special Features/Syndication Sales.

The **Theory I** experts regret that Professor Hall does not qualify for a Certificate of Achievement in **Theory I** Management.

RULE 5

Employees are not people (EANP)

Example 1

MANAGER #1: How many people work for you?
MANAGER #2: 3.7 FTE's* and 2.9 PTE's*.
 How many people work for you?
MANAGER #1: Two assistant directors and the girls.

EANP Example 2

MANAGER: *(Answering the phone with an artificial cheeriness.)* Thank you for calling KraftHouse in Merry Mart Mall. May I help you?
DICK: Could I speak to George Thomas? He's one of your clerks.
MANAGER: I'll have to have him call you.
DICK: Is he with a customer?
MANAGER: No.
DICK: This is his dad. I need to speak to him for just a moment.
MANAGER: *(Cheerfully)* I'll have to have him call you.
DICK: In the next few minutes?
MANAGER: Yes.
DICK: Fine. Here's my number. It's long distance. 813-555-5614. Hotel room 2222.

*FTE = Full-Time Equivalent
*PTE = Part-Time Equivalent

MANAGER: *(Sugary sweet.)* All right. I'll tell him. Thank you for calling KraftHouse. Abbagooday.

(Fifty-minute pause. Now Dick has a problem. He has to leave the hotel for a meeting, but George will hear that his dad is looking for him, call back and not reach him, and wonder if there is a family crisis. The call is simply to tell George, a theater major, that his dad is going to see a play that evening and to ask for "theater appreciation" tips. Dick calls back.)

MANAGER: *(With artificial cheeriness.)* Thank you for calling KraftHouse in Merry Mart Mall. May I help you?

DICK: This is George Thomas' dad again.

MANAGER: *(Cheerfully)* I'll have to have him call . . .

DICK: Never mind. It was nothing urgent. Please cancel the message and tell him not to worry.

MANAGER: *(Very cheerfully, having won.)* Fine. I'll tell him. Abbagooday.

Epilogue

Note 1: George's next evaluation indicated that he was a very valuable, hard-working employee. George used the evaluation as a reference when he went to work elsewhere.

Note 2: This company has now filed bankruptcy and is no longer in business.

RULE 6

Never listen to employees (NLTE)

At a casual restaurant/bar in Florida:

CUSTOMER: There used to be more people in here.
WAITRESS: I know. It's been slow since management let the guitar player go to save money.
CUSTOMER: Really?
WAITRESS: Yeah. They don't think that's what it is, but I do. Management isn't here talking to the customers all the time like I do.

RULE 7

Discourage innovative underlings (DIU)

As soon as a manager has tried everything conventional, he or she is entitled to say, "Gosh, I've tried everything."

Besides . . .

Innovative underlings cause job insecurity. For you!

So . . .

Solicit ideas from employees. Call it "input." Thank everyone for their ideas, then use your own.

Because . . .
- Analyzing input takes time (see Rule 1).
- Employees don't understand the risks involved in being innovative.

Theory I experts often add: But, keep a file of employees' ideas. When (s)he quits, the idea is yours.

RULE 8

Be inconsistent

- Change expectations daily. Reprimand the employee today for failure to meet today's expectations yesterday.
- Tell one employee (s)he can't take time off because his/her uncle died. Tell another it's okay to take time off to run a marathon.

RULE 9

Use every situation to your own advantage

Example 1

If you manage a restaurant, post a sign that says:

PLEASE WAIT TO BE SEATED

Then . . . Make 'em wait.

"Wait" means wait for as long as the host(ess) wants to make you wait.

Some people don't understand this and must be spoken to sharply when they become impatient.

Example 2

SAVE ENERGY
TURN OFF LIGHTS

Encourage people to be energy-conscious, and pocket the savings.

Example 3

Saying, "I'll be right with you" is an adequate substitute for prompt service.

RULE 10

Today's bottom line is the only consideration

Example 1

In one hospital:

MEMORANDUM

From: Dr. Hart, M.D., Chairman, Critical Care Committee
To: Hospital Administration
RE: Transfer of patients from the Emergency Room to the Coronary Care Unit.

It has come to my attention that patients admitted to the Coronary Care Unit from the Emergency Department are frequently taken to the X-ray Department first for their routine chest film. My understanding is that this is done because, under the DRG* payment system, X-rays done while the patient is still technically an outpatient can be charged for separately, thus producing more revenue to the hospital.

In my opinion, this delay in admission to the CCU presents:

- danger to the patients
- potential liability for the hospital.

I recommend discontinuation of this policy.

*DRG = Diagnosis-Related Groups—The current system for deciding how much hospitals are paid by Medicaid/Medicare and insurance companies.

Example 2

In another hospital:

PATIENT TO CT-SCAN TECHNICIAN: I don't understand. Why are you scanning my neck? My doctor ordered a scan of my low back.
BUSY CT-SCAN TECHNICIAN: Don't worry, sir. They're both the same price.

The **Theory I** experts say: Trust and Rule 10 are incompatible, even when dealing with hospitals, doctors, and others once considered "professional."

RULE 11

Ignore learning to write better letters and memos

Even though letters, reports, and memos are your primary means of corporate communication, learning to accurately express your thoughts in writing is a waste of time.

After all, if learning to write was necessary, they would have taught you that while you were in school.

RULE 12

Jump on bandwagons

They must be going somewhere.

RULE 13

Be insensitive

Remember: The customer is not one of "us." Do your best to make the customer feel like an intruder.

If you are:	**Then:**
A sales clerk in a department store	Argue with fellow clerks in front of customers about who is supposed to work this Saturday. Even if this customer decides to shop the competition, your work schedule is more important.
A flight attendant	Chat with the off-duty flight attendant about the vacation he is on, instead of responding to the first class passenger who wonders if you will hang up his coat.
Anyone who deals directly with customers	While ignoring the customer, continue discussing who goes on early lunch and who goes on late lunch, including details of who went early or late yesterday and the day before.

RULE 14

Never listen to consumers (NLTC)

Unsolicited comment of a Fayetteville, Arkansas, taxi driver:

(Disgustedly) Guarantees. Phhht! What are they worth? A washing machine, or a toaster, or a car. They tell it's absolutely guaranteed for a year. Then, if something goes wrong, instead of saying, 'Yes, sir, we'll fix it,' they say, 'Well, you know, that's just the nature of the thing.' Or they say, 'Sure, we'll fix it for you, but it'll take seven months to get the part.'

The **Theory I** experts say: Don't pay any attention to this man. He's only a taxi driver.

A disturbing contrast:

We know how to tinker, and we know how to listen, and that counts for a lot.
 —*Hartley and Melia Peavey*
  Peavey Electronics Corp.

Annual sales of Peavey Electronics: Nearly $100 million.   (Source: *INC Magazine*)

RULE 15

Always be on the phone (ABOP)

Example 1

CASHIER: *(Into phone while ringing up a sale on the cash register.)*
Yeah? No kiddin'! *(Slight pause.)* Yeah?! I mean, REALLY! The nerve. That'll be two-seventy-one. *(long pause.)*
(To customer, louder.)
I said, that'll be two-seventy-one. You got exact change?
CUSTOMER: *(Digging into his pocket.)*
I'll see. I might have the penny.
CASHIER: *(Into phone.)* He did?
CUSTOMER: I haven't got a penny.
CASHIER: *(Into phone.)* Don't worry about it.
CUSTOMER: The penny?
CASHIER: *(Handing customer some coins.)* Twenny-nine cen's your change. *(Into phone.)* Naw, don't worry about it. That'll be nin'y-eight cen's.
NEXT CUSTOMER: Are you talking to me?

ABOP Example 2

SUBORDINATE: May I speak to Mr. Big?
RECEPTIONIST: He's on another line.
SUBORDINATE: I'll hold.

Receptionist: It's likely to be a long call.
Subordinate: I really need to ask him this right now.
Receptionist: Please hold.
(Recorded music.)
Receptionist: He suggests you ask a Mr. Small.
Subordinate: I am Mr. Small.

Chapter 2

Insane Negativism

RULE 16

That's not my job (TNMJ)

Example 1

BOARD OF DIRECTORS: Our expectations were quite clear. These low quarterly earnings are not acceptable.

CORPORATE OFFICE: Our communication of the Board's earnings goals was quite explicit. But we don't personally generate sales.

REGIONAL OFFICE: We've done everything to generate new customers. The District's hiring practices are weak.

DISTRICT OFFICE: We're hiring the best people available. But we don't do the training.

STORE MANAGER: My employees are well-trained. These sales expectations are ridiculous.

EMPLOYEE: Hey, I'm just here for the paycheck.

TNMJ Example 2

I know this store sold it to you, but you'll have to discuss your problem with the manufacturer.

TNMJ Example 3

The air conditioner in your new "Waterview" condominium doesn't work? I'm sales only. Take it up with Maintenance. When? He comes to this complex every other Friday.

TNMJ Example 4

I wouldn't know who gave your father the medicine he's allergic to. I didn't come on 'til three.

TNMJ Example 5

Don't ask me how your bag ended up in Las Vegas (LAS) instead of Los Angeles (LAX).

TNMJ Example 6

"I'D POUR YOU MORE COFFEE, HONEY, BUT THIS ISN'T MY TABLE!"

RULE 17

Always be critical (ABC)

- Find fault with everything.
- Never be congratulatory to subordinates.
- If the work is good, take credit for it with your superiors after being critical of your subordinates.
- At annual evaluation time, never give a perfect score.

RULE 18

Use Theory I *methods to communicate criticism*

For example:

- Nastygrams — Letters which couple angry criticism with threats to fire the employee.
- Oral threats — Used when managers fear legal repercussions of the nastygram.
- Nasty brags — Stories exemplifying power and control over others, such as the last time you sent a job-conscious, frightened employee home in tears.
- Shocking and intimidating 4-letter words — Practice them in the mirror, with appropriate sneers, grimaces, and smirks, at least ten times each day.

RULE 19

Subordinates are inferior

Often, the most devastating assumption is that subordinates are innately inferior to those who have authority over them.

> —Dr. James Carr
> "The Boss is Dead, Long Live the Leader". (Reprint permission PACE magazine, the Piedmont Airlines inflight magazine, Pace Communications, Inc., Greensboro, NC)

The **Theory I** experts say: Poor, misled Dr. Carr. This assumption is not devastating. Subordinates are inferior. So's your spouse.

Note: This rule is related to the fact that many effective **Theory I** managers—men and women—are divorced.

RULE 20

Don't be distracted by productivity and quality

Your time should be spent as follows:

60% Fearing failure, reprimand, and termination
10% Doing the job
30% Re-doing the job

RULE 21

Force compliance with company policy regarding working hours

Example 1

A mail carrier was fired for breaking the rule that he should take five hours to finish his route. He often finished (without error) in three hours, had a leisurely lunch, then assisted his wife, an eight-year postal veteran, with her route.

His wife was fired, too, because it was against the rules to accept her husband's help.

Example 2

The **Theory I** distribution manager tells his route salesmen, "Skip the low-volume accounts. We can't afford overtime."

The company's president reports to the board:
- Overtime payroll costs—Zero
- Number of accounts—Constant
- Total sales—Stagnant
- Complaints—Increased
- Cause—Unknown

RULE 22

Never appreciate and enjoy what you have; agitate for more

In 1985, major league baseball was in the middle of one of its best seasons. Weather did not force cancellation of a major league game until mid-May. Pete Rose electrified the nation by breaking Ty Cobb's record of 4,191 hits. Tom Seaver got his 300th career victory. Rod Carew got his 3,000th major league hit. By the All-Star break (halfway through the season), attendance figures showed that an average of 33,000 people (!) attended each major league game.

The average salary for baseball players had reached the unbelievable figure of $215,000 per year, not counting endorsements for shaving on television, modeling underwear, etc.

How to maintain and build on this fabulous success?

The answer was obvious: Strike. So they did.

RULE 23

Always be defensive (ABD)

(11:00 p.m., at The Hotel)

TIRED TRAVELER: The room you just checked me into is already occupied.

DESK CLERK: I didn't check you in.

TIRED TRAVELER: I've been checked into a room that's already occupied.

DESK CLERK: I didn't do it. I just came on.

TIRED TRAVELER: I'm not after anybody's job. I know these things happen. I just want to get checked into an unoccupied room, okay?

DESK CLERK: *(Sigh.)* Well, I'll try to find you one. *(While searching for a room on his computer, yells in the direction of the inner office.)* Hey, Charlie, did you check this guy in?

TIRED TRAVELER: Could I see the manager?

DESK CLERK: You're lookin' at him.

RULE 24

Always be secretive (ABS)

And I Was There (by Rear Admiral Edwin T. Layton, Captain Roger Pineau, and John Costello, Morrow Books, 1985.), a book by two retired Naval officers and a British historian, claims that Admiral Husband E. Kimmel, former commander of the U.S. Naval Fleet at Pearl Harbor, was made the scapegoat for Japan's infamous attack on December 7, 1941.

It now appears, says the book, that Kimmel did not ignore warnings from Washington, as had been claimed. Neither is it necessary to speculate that President Franklin D. Roosevelt knew of the impending Japanese attack, but did nothing because he wanted the United States to declare war on the Axis.

And I Was There proposes the theory that bitter feuding existed between the Navy's intelligence organization and its high command. Bureaucratic infighting—the reluctance to share information—could have been a major factor in Japan's success with the element of surprise!

The **Theory I** experts say: If ABS works for the military, it'll work for you.

Theory I experts create SNAFU's* by telling only one person what's going on, when three need to know.

*SNAFU: A World War II term meaning "Situation Normal: All Fouled Up."

RULE 25

Truth in advertising has no market value

Check with your legal counsel about how far you can
- hype your own product
- knock the competition

without losing lawsuits filed by

- quality-conscious consumers and
- knocked competitors.

The best **Theory I** managers ignore lawsuits and simply budget for out-of-court settlements.

RULE 26

Never admit a mistake (NAAM)

Only weaklings admit mistakes.

Note: Richard M. Nixon qualifies for a special Certificate of Achievement in **Theory I** management.

RULE 27

Stupid questions don't deserve an answer, and most questions are stupid

Ask any question you like.

We won't answer.

RULE 28

Follow the GGG Credo

Always be:
- **Grumpy**
- **Grabby**
- **Greedy**

Example: The City of New York

"Whenever a man goes into the city, he deserves whatever happens to him there."

—Horace Van der Gelder,
Hello Dolly, the Movie

RULE 29

The Golden Rule is religious only— it has no business applications

Someone may tell you that courtesy, sensitivity, and concern for other peoples' problems are good for business. This is nonsense.

RULE 30

Live by the Mobile Golden Rule (MGR)

| MOBILE GOLDEN RULE | Do to him what they did to you before he does to you what the others did to him. |

Example 1

The hotel you stayed in last night screwed up. This hotel will surely do the same. Stomp up to the counter and bark, "My name's Thompson and you damn well better have my reservation!" (See also ABD, Rule 23).

MGR Example 2

Our Chicago cab driver told us all about the problems with the cab business in Chicago.

A cab driver must drive eight to ten hours a day to break even because of the high daily charge to lease a cab, plus fuel costs.

Therefore, cab drivers feel the company is ripping them off, so it's okay for the drivers to rip off somebody else—namely the passenger.

The **Theory I** experts wonder: Could this be the Mobile Golden Rule in action?

Additional Note: This cab driver (he claimed) is one of three who sued the City of Chicago and the cab company for (trebled) antitrust damages of $400 million.

The **Theory I** experts wonder: Is it coincidental that the abbreviation for Mobile Golden Rule (MGR) is the same as the abbreviation for manager?

Chapter 3

I
N
SUPERFICIALITY
A
N
E

RULE 31

The successful business relies on a computer that draws colored graphs

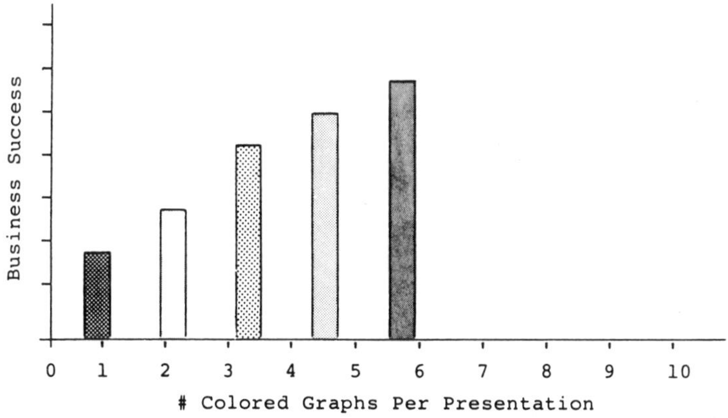

RULE 32

Money is the only motivation

Practical applications:
- Your raise and bonus are more important than the company.
- The company is more important than the customer.
- Just before the company folds, revise your résumé and go where they'll pay you what you're worth.

RULE 33

Oppose tax reform

Go for that tax shelter. It won't make you any money. It may even lose some. But the important thing is, you are giving your money to someone other than the government.

RULE 34

Sweat the small stuff (STSS)

Example 1

Limit the number of clients you work for so you will have time to nit-pick your expense reports.

STSS/Example 2

A full day's work is revising the work schedule, re-inventorying and reordering needed supplies, updating your résumé, and clearing off your desk before you go home.

RULE 35

Expect "the system" to work

You bought "the system." They said it would make you an outstanding manager. If it doesn't work for you, "the system" is to blame. Go buy another one.

The **Theory I** experts agree: This is especially true of data systems.

RULE 36

Expect "communication" to be automatic

Don't help people comprehend. If they don't understand now, they never will.

So:
- Never send any copies of your letters to people who might need to know what you're thinking.
- Never insist that different factions meet together.
- Never include detractors in your communications with others. Hide communications from detractors—try to put one over.
- Never ask:
  - Why did you ask?
  - Was my answer to the point?
  - Do you understand?

RULE 37

Never have one person do what four people can do

This
- lowers the unemployment rate
- creates a hot market for "communications" seminars
- puts you one up in the "How-many-people-report-to-you?" derby.

RULE 38

If a form is confusing, print a lengthy explanation of how to fill out the form, instead of improving the form

Example

Dear Taxpayer:

Through our monitoring program at the service centers, we have found that a significant number of Federal Tax Deposit (FTD) coupons are not properly completed. Incorrect preparation of the coupons will result in your payments being misapplied. The FTD coupons and instructions were revised in August 1984 to help prevent this problem.

The two most common errors on incorrectly prepared coupons are:

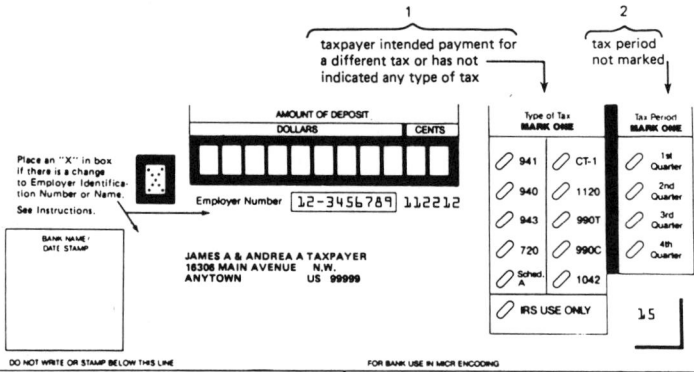

1 — taxpayer intended payment for a different tax or has not indicated any type of tax

2 — tax period not marked

[Sample FTD coupon form for JAMES A & ANDREA A TAXPAYER, 16306 MAIN AVENUE N.W., ANYTOWN US 99999, Employer Number 12-3456789, amount 112212]

Obviously these errors are costly for us and for you, not only in dollars but also in the extra time you must spend responding to an IRS inquiry.

You can help eliminate these costs by alerting your preparers and urging them to submit these forms correctly the FIRST TIME.

Notice 736 (5-85)   Department of the Treasury - Internal Revenue Service

RULE 39

Create the illusion that your products are dependable

When building automobiles, "dependability" means putting in a mileage indicator with six digit places instead of five.

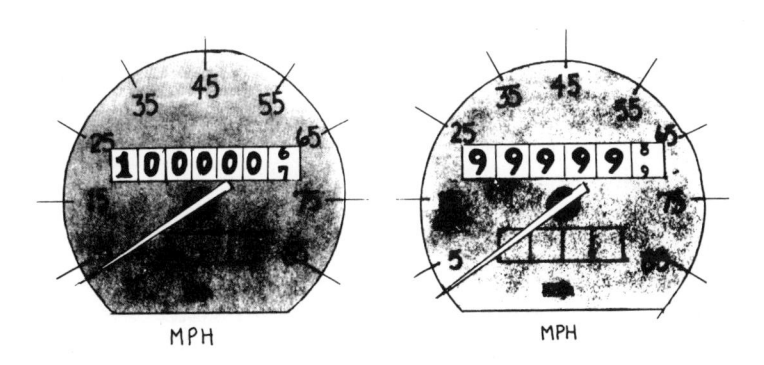

MPH   MPH

RULE 40

Let the logistics beat you

Example: You must prepare a working draft for discussion before the next meeting of the task force. Just as you put the finishing touches on the draft, forty-eight hours before the meeting, a senior member of the task force adds input that he insists be included.

Now you have a production problem.

What to do?

You could:

- Have avoided the problem by clearly stating a deadline and expecting everyone to meet it.
- Obtain temporary clerical help—an extra expense.
- Expect your secretary to do the extra typing, overtime, without extra pay.
- Learn to use the word processor yourself. But that's not in your job description.
- Avoid delay by sending the revised material overnight mail. Nonsense. Overnight mail costs extra and is often not read with the urgency felt by the sender.

Use **Theory I!**

- Put the material into the secretarial pool to be typed, whenever.

- Postpone the meeting for three, maybe four, weeks which is probably the next time everybody can get together.
- Blame the ultimate failure of the project on the person who provided the slow input, and try to get promoted to his/her position.

RULE 41

Beware of promises which the consumer expects you to keep

Example 1

Quality is job one? Grow up! Selling is job one. And you want to be number one at job one. You haven't got time to worry about keeping promises to the customer.

Example 2

OFFICE MANAGER: *(On the phone to the salesperson)* We need an acoustic cover for our noisy printer.
SALES REP: Of course. No problem.
OFFICE MANAGER: How much are they?
SALES REP: About $400.00.
OFFICE MANAGER: We'll be moving soon and we'd like to get it before . . .
SALES REP: No problem. I'll come by.
(Later, in the office.)
SALES REP: Oh, **that** model printer. That'll be closer to $500.00.
OFFICE MANAGER: *(Less enthusiastic)* When will it be delivered?
SALES REP: Two, three weeks—five at the outside. Unless, of course . . .
OFFICE MANAGER: *(Unenthusiastically)* But you said we could get it by . . .

Sales Rep: Could I use your phone? I'll get you an exact quote.
(Returning from phone.)
Including the delivery charge—$685.00.
Office Manager: Forget it.

Note effective use of **Theory I** principles by the sales rep.

- Quoting lower-than-low price gets foot in door.
- Promising immediate delivery is no problem to the sales rep, who is not responsible for delivery.

Ignore the fact that the sales rep lost the sale. He encountered a rare office manager who has not read this book.

RULE 42

Create a consumer expectations gap (CEG) between you and your customers

> Consumer Expectations Gap (CEG) means the consumer's frustration created by simultaneous emphases in American business management:
> - Hype advertising
> - Cost control by reducing product quality and/or customer services.

Our ability to market ourselves substantially outstrips our ability to deliver services.

—Vice President of Marketing and Community Relations at Major Medical Center

RULE 43

When the consultant leaves, photocopy and adopt

Do not discuss, adapt, modify, or change the consultant's recommendations or written materials. Avoid thought. After all, what are consultants for? They should provide instant, off-the-shelf, easy solutions. When a solution fails, it's the consultant's fault.

RULE 44

Don't read (DR)

Are you still reading this book? Caution. Your Certificate of Achievement in **Theory I** management will be withheld.

Books are confusing. They make you think. Now—pay attention—managers do not have time to think.

Never mind that the reading material may be instructions for proper completion of your assigned task.

RULE 45

When faced with lack of productivity, hold a meeting

Meeting to discuss decreased productivity beats working.

The meeting's content should be ambiguous and vague, rather than providing step-by-step suggestions for increasing productivity.

Meanwhile, use your computer that draws colored graphs (see Rule 31) to create the illusion of productivity.

RULE 46

Never do in a conference call what you can do by paying travel expenses for a meeting in a remote location

RULE 47

Beware of old-fashioned definitions of "work"

Antique definition of work:

Work is the necessary effort required to effectively accomplish specific tasks and objectives.

Contemporary definitions of work:

- Work is that which is done only if there is no other way to finance racquetball club memberships, jogging outfits, Walkmans, and Heineken.
- Work is frenzied activity in the presence of one's boss.

RULE 48

Always look busy (ALB)

A **Theory I** contributor (MKB) contributes:

When I worked for the police department, I had a watch commander who was aware that I finished my work three times faster than my coworkers.

So, he let me visit other departments. But, to avoid getting flak from the brass, he instructed me to always "carry a clipboard, walk briskly, and look busy."

RULE 49

If the method doesn't work, attack the concept

When you arrive at Point C, assume that the person with the good idea was wrong. Never consider that you might have selected the wrong method.

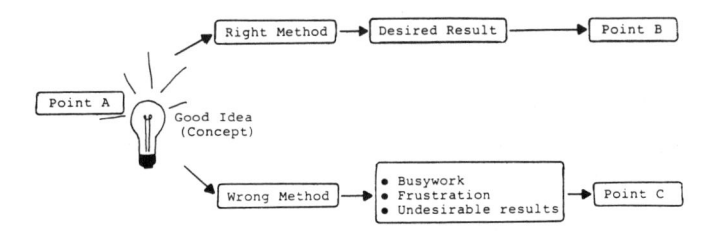

```
                    ┌──────────────┐   ┌────────────────┐      ┌─────────┐
                  ▶ │ Right Method │──▶│ Desired Result │─────▶│ Point B │
                 /  └──────────────┘   └────────────────┘      └─────────┘
┌─────────┐    \|/
│ Point A │    💡  Good Idea
└─────────┘        (Concept)
                 \
                  \ ┌──────────────┐   ┌─────────────────────┐   ┌─────────┐
                  ▶ │ Wrong Method │──▶│ • Busywork          │──▶│ Point C │
                    └──────────────┘   │ • Frustration       │   └─────────┘
                                       │ • Undesirable results│
                                       └─────────────────────┘
```

RULE 50

Go Through The Motions (GTTM)

GTTM is the hub of **Theory** I.

Example 1: Communicating with the Public

CLERK: Welcome to Burger World. May I take your order?
CUSTOMER: Yes, I'll have three hamburgers, three shakes, and seven fries to go.
CLERK: Three Globals! Would you like any fries with that?
CUSTOMER: Yes. Seven.
CLERK: Three Globals, seven fries! How about a beverage drink with that?
CUSTOMER: I'd like three shakes.
CLERK: Three Globals, seven fries, three shakes! Is that for here or to go?
CUSTOMER: To go.
CLERK: Thank you. Drive through, and abbagooday!

Example 2: The Theory I Work Day at the Office

9:00 a.m.	Arrive at the office. Make coffee. Tell everyone what you did over the weekend.

9:30-9:50 a.m.	Figure out where you were at quitting time on Friday.
9:50-10:30 a.m.	Work time (30 productive minutes).
10:30-10:50 a.m.	Coffee Break
10:50-11:10 a.m.	Figure out where you were before Break.
11:10-11:45 a.m.	Work time (30 productive minutes).
11:45 a.m.-Noon	Discuss where to have lunch.
Noon-1:00 p.m.	Lunch
1:00-1:30 p.m.	Return to the office. Make coffee for the afternoon. Finish lunchtime discussion.
1:30-1:45 p.m.	Figure out where you were before lunch.
1:45-2:30 p.m.	Work time (45 productive minutes).
2:30-2:45 p.m.	Afternoon Break
2:45-3:00 p.m.	Figure out where you were before the break.
3:00-4:00 p.m.	Lengthiest work time of the day (60 productive minutes).
4:00-4:15 p.m.	Personal phone calls. Decide where to go for supper.

4:15-4:30 p.m.   Prepare request for additional staff.

4:30 p.m.   Leave the office.

GTTM Example 3: Product Reliability

JANE: I'm from Honest Olds. There's an urgent recall on your car.
ME: There must be some mistake. I've driven it for 2½ years without any problems.
JANE: But you didn't respond to the recalls.
ME: I didn't get a recall notice.
JANE: I'll make a note of that.
ME: Wouldn't I have had trouble by now?
JANE: Not necessarily.
ME: What are they?
JANE: 83CO4 and 83EO1.
ME: What?
JANE: Those are the two recalls.
ME: What are they?
JANE: 83CO4 and . . .
ME: What does that mean?
JANE: Ummm. One of them is a bracket on a brake—or something like that. I think.
ME: What?

JANE: Well, let me look it up for sure. *(Pause.)* Oh, no. 83CO4 is not that, 83CO4 is the engine coolant fan relay.
ME: What's the other one?
JANE: 83EO1.
ME: I mean, what does that mean?
JANE: I think it's a bracket . . . no, that's the vacuum hose.
ME: Could you just read me what it says?
JANE: EGR vacuum source hoses may be plugged.
ME: Okay. But I didn't get this car from Honest Olds. I lease it and the leasing company got it from Elsewhere Olds.
JANE: Why didn't you say so?
(Later, at the dealer:)
"SERVICE COORDINATOR": Oh, yes. One of those. We'll take care of it.
ME: What's the problem?
SERVICE COORDINATOR: Oh, sometimes there are defects in the engineering of the cars. What they screw up, we fix.
ME: It might be better for everybody to just not screw up in the first place.
SERVICE COORDINATOR: Yeah. I guess that's why Mercedes does so well.

GTTM Example 4: Corporate Credo

Welcome to Deregulated Airlines.

You have free mileage credits, King-of-the-Hill Club treatment, free booze, and advance seat assignment.

But, your flight has been cancelled.

Welcome to Hilltop Hospital.

The hot food is hot. The cold food is cold. The customer relations representative welcomes your comments.

Unfortunately, we're a little short on nursing help since the layoffs, so get your own wheelchair.

GTTM: A Disturbing Exception

Evaluating the Chicago Bears halfway through the 1985 season, Dick Butkus said, "You don't see any going through the motions with these Bears."

Note: The Chicago Bears won the National Football Conference Central Division, the National Football Conference Championship, and the 1986 Super Bowl.

The **Theory I** experts say: Neither Dick Butkus nor the Chicago Bears qualify for **Theory I** Certificates of Achievement.

But you tell 'em.

Chapter 4

I
N
S
Artificiality
N
E

RULE 51

When it comes to your title, be a tough negotiator

Example 1

You are not a grocery chain checkout clerk. You are a "Qualified Career Associate Scanning Professional."

Example 2

Nurses have achieved the most advancement in title:

Year	Title
1950s	Chief Nurse
1960s	Director of Nursing Services
1970s	Administrator of Nursing Services
1980s	Vice President of Patient Care Resources
1990s	??? New Heights ???

RULE 52

Never call a spade a spade

- A beauty shop is not a beauty shop. It is an "image salon."
- A lie in advertising is a "legally, socially, and professionally acceptable application of general marketing principles."
- A clerk is a "Sales Associate."
- A problem is an "opportunity."
- Add your favorite examples:

RULE 53

Let television dictate your lifestyle

- If you have ring-around-the-collar, change detergents instead of washing your neck.
- Develop a short attention span.
- All activities start on the hour or on the half hour.
- If you don't see it on the 10 o'clock news, it's not important.

RULE 54

Apply sports maxims directly and absolutely to the business world

- There is no value in being No. 2.
- Nice guys finish last.
- "Winning is the only thing." (Absolute business translation = Rule 32: Money is the only motivation.)
- Let's see that on instant replay.

RULE 55

Never communicate directly (NCD)

The **Theory I** manager must budget for agents, attorneys, and other third parties.

Example: Carlos May, former baseball player, is only one of many ball players who have brought suit against their agents, charging breach of contract and mishandling of funds. According to May's suit, $50,000 of his money was invested in tax shelters that "went sour." Other such players include Ron Guidry, New York Yankees' pitcher, who reportedly lost more than $3 million, and outfielder George Foster of the Mets, who reputedly lost $825,000 in just one deal. And, Wayne Gretzky, of the Edmonton Oilers, tried to recover $400,000 of the $500,000 he lost in a real estate investment deal, suggested by his investment advisor, who also owned part of the real estate company.

Practical Application: Each **Theory I** manager should strive to become the manager of a professional athlete.

RULE 56

Believe in the adversary process

An actual personalized license plate:

RULE 57

The corporate myth isn't just for tax purposes—believe it!

You go into business for yourself. First, you establish the paper corporation, for tax purposes. You are now President of yourself.

Next, the president needs a large office. (Big bucks for rent.) Its furnishings must be tasteful. (Big bucks for furniture.) The foyer requires a cultured "administrative assistant." (Big bucks for salary.) The myth is now complete. Bills exceed initial revenues. The company never has a chance to succeed. You fold.

The **Theory I** experts agree: That's okay. It's all the government's fault.

RULE 58

Take a bureaucratic approach to any task

Theory I cake-baking procedure:

Step 1: Appoint the Cake Committee.
Step 2: Hire the Cake Coordinator to staff the Cake Committee.
Step 3: Develop a written plan. Don't call it "recipe." Name it "Long-Range Plan for Development and Implementation of Cake-Baking Objectives."
Step 4: Establish a confidentiality policy for the Cake Committee.
Step 5: Hire an attorney to review the confidentiality policy.
Step 6: Establish a system of agendas, meetings, minutes, and progress reports for the Cake Committee.
Step 7: Stay away from the kitchen!

Chapter 5

INSANE NERDNESS

Nerdness is a combination of two or more **Theory I** rules to create a new rule.

RULE 59

Solve your problem, not the customer's

The 7:00 a.m. flight on Deregulated Airlines was cancelled. Mechanical problems. The following scene ensued:

TICKET AGENT: No problem, sir, there is a later flight at 7:50 a.m.
PASSENGER: That will make my 8:40 connection to Chicago?
TICKET AGENT: Oh, you're going on to Chicago? No. But we can put you on another connection. *(Handing the passenger a ticket.)* Here you are. I've put your new schedule right on there for you.

THE NEW SCHEDULE					
	Flight 2355	10Jan	LV 7:50a	AR	9:05a
Other airline:	Flight 677	10Jan	LV 9:14a	AR	10:45a

PASSENGER: That's a nine-minute connection. Are these gates right together?
TICKET AGENT: No.
PASSENGER: On the same concourse?
TICKET AGENT: No. *(Pause.)* But it's not a really long walk. *(Pause.)* Besides, there are tailwinds this morning and I'm sure you'll get there earlier than the scheduled time.

PASSENGER: Is there any other choice?
TICKET AGENT: No.

The **Theory I** experts agree: An ingenious maneuver, utilizing Rules 16, 30, and 42.

RULE 60

Wait for complaints before making adjustments

Example:

A Chicago commuter train line received complaints of trains running late. Their response (paraphrased) was:

First, you know, we had that wreck a couple of months ago. Therefore, trains that were taking 35 mph speed limit curves at 45 mph are now taking them at 25 mph. No way can we expect them to stay on schedule.

And, we've had a 50% increase in ridership in the last two years, probably as a result of our excellent marketing campaign. That has slowed down our trains by increasing loading time at each stop.

The **Theory I** experts agree: An effective blend of Rules 23, 25, and 42.

RULE 61

To get more money, threaten disruptive action

Example:

Richard Dent had a superb year as a defensive end on the (1986 Super Bowl Champion) Chicago Bears football team. During the NFL playoffs, Dent's agent threatened to hold him out of the Super Bowl unless a contract dispute was settled.

Coach Mike Ditka's response was, "If his agent doesn't play, that won't hurt us."

Note: Dent played in the Super Bowl and was named Most Valuable Player.

The **Theory I** experts agree: An ingenious combination of Rules 13, 22, 28, and 55.

RULE 62

Loyalty has no market value

In a TV interview (January 7, 1986), Dave Debusschere, who had just been fired as General Manager of the New York Knicks basketball team, said that losing his job wasn't so bad, because he had become frustrated by a conglomerate company.

It was difficult, he explained, to make effective and timely decisions when he had to await approval from several layers of management . . . especially when some of these managers were "on their boat" and unavailable to him for a period of days.

The **Theory I** experts agree: A practical application of Rules 5, 13, and 58.

Special Note: The fact that Dave Debusschere was a local hero as a New York Knicks player is irrelevant. "Loyalty" is expected of employees. But managers can't afford the luxury of loyalty.

RULE 63

Be arrogantly aggressive, even if it hurts your cause

Some say militant feminism, which eventually alienated and embarrassed many women, may well be dying. But women's rights is a critical and important issue, with many in support of lasting social change.

The **Theory I** experts (and their wives) agree: Militant feminism was a blend of Rules 3 and 23.

But we also agree: Chauvinism abounds in business.

Until recently, Ace was the place with no helpful hardware women.

RULE 64

If "no" doesn't work, show your muscle

In Ithaca, New York, an employee was fired for fighting a policy of charging employees 10¢ for a glass of ice water. The company's executive director said the policy was implemented because too many employees were asking cafeteria workers for cups of ice water and cafeteria workers couldn't get the meals served on time. "We tried saying 'no,'" he said. "That simply didn't work."

The **Theory I** experts agree: Prime candidate for Nerd of the Year.

RULE 65

Nerdness can be corporate

According to the *Arkansas Gazette,* Reynolds Metals Company decided to shut down its aluminum production plant in Arkansas because, they said, of the rising cost of energy, as well as slackening aluminum demand.

Prior to their pull-out, the company had been a key player in joining the State of Arkansas and Arkansas Power & Light in solving cost problems related to the operation of one location (the Grand Gulf Power Plant). The result was, basically, that Arkansas Power users paid higher rates.

Reynolds' enthusiastic role in that issue led state officials to think the company planned a long future in Arkansas. But a close look at the settlement revealed that deferment of much of the Grand Gulf cost burden to rate payers would be in later years, after Reynolds had left the state (and would, therefore, not be affected, as a corporate user, by the higher rates).

Arkansas turned its attention to providing services for the resulting dislocated workers and their families, including job retraining.

The **Theory I** experts agree: Corporate nerdness is the best kind because you can frustrate many groups of people all at once.

Chapter 6

Insane Ego

The ego! The electricity that gives life to the creature. Without ego, **Theory I** management could never have been born.

RULE 66

Beware of people who answer your questions

When holding a management retreat, it is important to choose facilitators who understand that:
- You do not really want answers. If answers existed, you would, of course, have found them yourself.
- What you do want is another circular bull session, resulting once again in the reassuring conclusion that the questions are really too difficult for anyone to answer.

RULE 67

Travel like you mean it

- Always fly first class. It's not the two free drinks for only $300. It's the image.
- Never check any baggage—carry on your entire wardrobe and three computers. (The experienced **Theory I** manager might consider shipping bags by overnight delivery service and charging it to the client.)
- If, while rushing through the airport, you get slowed down behind somebody with a cane, mumble, loud enough for them to hear, that they should stay home if they can't keep up with the fast-track pace.
- At the security checkpoint, choose the line with the most business suits. These are the frequent travelers who know the system, and the line will move much faster than the tourist line.
- When the flight attendant offers you a pillow or blanket, don't take one. Real men don't.
- Getting out of the rental car parking lot is a race, just like everything else. Be No. 1! (But try to avoid participating in the demolition derby being conducted by rental car employees.)
- Rent a car with a phone. Call clients, and remind them that you're always on the go.

RULE 68

Never worry about your arrogance tarnishing your public image

Example 1

STARS' FREQUENT DISAPPEARING ACTS CANCEL PUBLIC CONFIDENCE IN OPERA

On opening night of the current San Francisco opera season, Terrance A. McEwen went before the curtain to make an announcement. So familiar had these "curtain talks" become in recent years . . . that the audience groaned, bracing itself for the latest bad news. "I hate to break the tradition," said McEwen. "But tonight there are no cancellations. Everyone is here and well and will sing."

—by John von Rhein
(Copyrighted Dec. 1, 1985, Chicago Tribune Company. All rights reserved. Used with permission.)

A Contrasting Example: Opera star Marilyn Horne was asked if she feared competition from up and coming young singers. Ms. Horne replied that she doesn't worry about the competition . . . what she worries about is singing well and that when she does "those other things seem to pretty well take care of themselves."

Example 2

CONDO SALESMAN WITH 11 EMPTY UNITS: Better buy it today. I can't guarantee we won't sell out.
POTENTIAL CUSTOMER: I think we'll look elsewhere.

Example 3

RULE 69

Gatekeepers, use your power.
Make people wait at the gate

- If you're a toll booth attendant, take your time and always hold change and receipts barely out of reach.
- If you're a ticket agent, tell people to stay behind the line until you give them permission to step forward.
- If you're a clerk in the hospital finance office, take a lot of time completing the paperwork, and tell the patient not to bleed on your rug.
- If you're a waitress, give perfect service up until it's time for the check. Then disappear for 15 or 20 minutes.
- If you're a convenience store clerk, make the customer wait at the register while you finish mopping the floor.

RULE 70

Above all, never evaluate your own performance

Perfection requires no review.

Afterword

You really insisted on reading this book, didn't you? There's no hope for you as a **Theory I** manager because:
- You read.
- You finish what you start.

We suspect you may even support—

An Alternative

THE SENSSIBLE MANAGEMENT STYLE

1. Exchange amenities.
2. Promise a customer only what you intend to deliver.
3. Work on fixing the customer's problem, instead of working on fixing the blame for the customer's problem.
4. On your shift, work as though you are the only employee. Try not to punt customers' problems to the next shift.
5. Do things for motivations other than money.
6. Instead of envying the success of others, think about the fact that if you're in the same company, the success of others reflects well on you.
7. Encourage your people to represent the organization rather than making them resent it.
8. Keep your expectations and demands reasonable.
9. Recognize and reward loyalty.
10. Say, "Thank you."

Theory I *Glossary*

ABC Always Be Critical
ABD Always Be Defensive
ABOP Always Be On the Phone
ABS Always Be Secretive
ALB Always Look Busy
CEG Consumer Expectations Gap. The consumer's frustration created by simultaneous emphasis of American business management on [a] hype advertising and [b] cost control by reducing product quality and/or customer service.
DIU Discourage Innovative Underlings
DR Don't Read
EANP Employees Are Not People
GGG Credo: Always be Grumpy, Grabby, Greedy
GTTM Go Through The Motions
Half-Fast Manager A manager who tries to be fast track, but only half succeeds.
MGR Mobile Golden Rule. Do to him what they did to you before he does to you what the others did to him.
NAAM Never Admit A Mistake
NCD Never Communicate Directly
Nerdness The combination of any two or more **Theory I** rules to create a new rule.
NLTC Never Listen To Customers
NLTE Never Listen To Employees
STSS Sweat The Small Stuff
TNMJ That's Not My Job

ABOUT THE AUTHORS

Richard E. Thompson, M.D., a former pediatrician, is President of Thompson, Mohr & Associates, Inc., a healthcare-related management/leadership consulting firm based in Tarpon Springs, Florida.

David R. Thompson, a former middle-manager, is President of SENSS, Inc., a business-related publications/writing services/seminars firm based in San Antonio, Texas.

YOU CAN ORDER

*Personalized, Official Certificates of Achievement in **Theory I** Management*

Suitable for:
- Framing
- Awarding at banquet "roasts," or as "prizes" at company parties/picnics
- Giving to the boss—anonymously!

GREAT! Send me _____ personalized, official Certificates of Achievement in **Theory I** management. (Limit: 100 to a customer.)

Make the certificates out to:

_____
Name

_____
Title

_____   (Continue on back of this order form, or staple
Name   list to the order form.)

_____
Title

_____
Name

_____
Title

Amount Enclosed = $2.50 for each certificate
               (no additional postage
               or handling)
               TOTAL AMOUNT
               ENCLOSED $_____

_____
Your Name/Title

_____
Company

_____
Street or P.O. Box

_____
City, State, ZIP Code

Send this completed order form with payment to:
SENSS Publications and Seminars, Inc.
312 Florida Avenue North #344
Tarpon Springs, FL 33589

IF YOU ENJOYED *THEORY I*

- We welcome your reaction. Drop us a note.

- You are encouraged to return this form for information about the authors' availability:

  ☐ to speak at conventions, sales meetings, etc.

  ☐ to speak at company awards banquets

  ☐ to conduct one-day motivational workshops

  ☐ to conduct orientation and/or refresher training sessions

  ☐ to write training/procedure manuals

  ☐ to write items for your company newsletter.

Name

Title

Company

Street or P.O. Box

City, State, ZIP Code

Return completed form to:
    David R. Thompson, President
    SENSS Publications and Seminars, Inc.
    P.O. Box 47603
    San Antonio, Texas 78265